CLEAN BREAK

Clean Break in association with Arcola Theatre presents

T0190793

it felt empty when the heart went at first but it is alright now

by **Lucy Kirkwood**

First performed at Arcola Theatre, London
on Wednesday 7 October 2009

it felt empty when the heart went at first but it is alright now

by Lucy Kirkwood

Cast

DIJANA **Hara Yannas**
GLORIA **Madeline Appiah**

Creative Team

Writer **Lucy Kirkwood**
Director **Lucy Morrison**
Designer **Chloe Lamford**
Lighting Designer **Anna Watson**
Sound Designer **Becky Smith**

7–31 October 2009
Arcola Theatre, London
Box Office 020 7503 1646
www.arcolatheatre.com

Author's Note

In 2007 Lucy Morrison and I visited the Helen Bamber Foundation's extraordinary *Journey* exhibition in Trafalgar Square, and decided we had found the play we wanted to make together. I began researching, piecing together what I felt Dijana's own journey would be. I became particularly interested in Yarl's Wood Detention Centre, and have spent the past two years working with women in or leaving the criminal justice system and a lot of time thinking about what captivity does to you, the particular effects it has on women, their coping mechanisms and the kind of relationships they form. But the idea that someone might be incarcerated, punished for being the *victim* of crime was breathtaking to me.

But Lucy and I felt it important that this play was about a person, not a statistic. That sometimes, by dwelling (to the point of prurience, perhaps) on the visual spectacle of sexual abuses and physical torture, the real woman at the centre of the story sometimes becomes obscured by a language of track marks and dirty lingerie. She is denied again the chance to be anything but defined by this experience, anything *but* a victim.

Dijana *is* a victim of crime, a victim of gross inhumanity. But she is not a victim in herself. She has survived. She is broken, maybe to the point of irrepair, but she keeps going, she finds coping mechanisms, lies to herself, yes – but is still telling her own story, still trying to work out the world she finds herself in, still battling. In this way she is like any woman who finds her way into the criminal justice system, but especially like the women of the Poppy Project who so kindly gave of their time and themselves during the development of this play. One of the defining experiences of being rescued from sex traffic is storytelling. You tell your story again and again, to police, to lawyers, to caseworkers, to doctors, to counsellors. It was therefore an act of extreme generosity for these women to repeat their stories yet again for my benefit.

They weren't happy women. They were women who couldn't sleep with the lights off, women who told me that if they had a son they would not trust him, women who had had extensive dental surgery to correct the chronic grinding of their teeth (an effect of the Post Traumatic Stress Disorder they were suffering), women who jumped every time a Renault car drove past, women who lost their hair, women who lost their sight and women who had their ambitions and hopes used against them to the point that they had lost all ability to trust fully in another human being.

And yet. The women of the Poppy Project are still here. Still telling their stories. And while the problem of sex traffic is not going away – won't go away until we fully address that slavery is thriving in this country – with the help of remarkable organisations like Poppy and the Helen Bamber Foundation, the voices of these women are getting louder.

This play is dedicated to them.

Lucy Kirkwood was Clean Break's Resident Playwright from 2007–2009.

Cast, Creative and Production Team

Ali Beale (Production Manager)
Ali has worked in theatre, opera, dance, performance and installation, touring both nationally and internationally. Recent theatre credits include: *The Forest, Brilliant, And the Rain Falls Down, Fleet, Field of Miracles, Feast Your Eyes* (Fevered Sleep); *An Infinite Line* (Fevered Sleep – Brighton Festival); *Dancing Time, Camera Obscura* (David Harradine); *Performing Medicine, Sampled, Under Glass, Must, Fantastic Voyage* (The Clod Ensemble); *Give Us a Hand* (Little Angel Theatre); *Guided Tour* (Peter Reder – Gijon, Arizona, Singapore, Bucharest and Moscow); *The Evocation of Papa Mas, The Firework Maker's Daughter* (Told by an Idiot); *The Ratcatcher of Hamlin* (Cartoon De Salvo); *Gumbo Jumbo* (The Gogmagogs). For Clean Break, Ali has worked on *Black Crows, This Wide Night* and *Missing Out*.

Rachel Shipp (Production Manager)
Rachel is a production/technical manager specialising in small-scale theatre and dance. For six years she was Technical Manager at the ICA in London before pursuing a freelance career in 1996. In 2000 she took a year out and travelled the Pacific Rim from Hong Kong to Ecuador. Since then she has been touring extensively in the UK and worldwide. She has recently worked with Shobana Jeyasingh Dance Company, The Cholmondeleys and the Featherstonehaughs, Nigel Charnock, Bock and Vincenzi, East London Dance, Theatre Rites, Paines Plough and Akram Khan.

Chloe Lamford (Designer)
Chloe Lamford trained in Theatre Design at Wimbledon School of Art. Design for theatre includes: *Sus* (Young Vic); *Everything Must Go* (Soho Theatre); *This Wide Night* (Clean Break, Soho Theatre and tour); *The Mother Ship, How to Tell the Monsters from the Misfits* (Birmingham Rep); *Blithe Spirit* (Watermill Theatre); *The Snow Queen* (Sherman Theatre, Cardiff); *Antigone at Hell's Mouth* (Kneehigh Theatre and NYT at the Soho Theatre); *Silence* (NYT); *Lola* (Trestle Theatre Company); *Small Miracle* (Tricycle Theatre and Mercury Theatre, Colchester); *Blue Sky State, Soul Play* (Mercury Theatre, Colchester); *The Wild Party* (Rosie Kay Dance Company); *The Good Person of Sichuan* (Birmingham); *The Shy Gas Man* (Southwark Playhouse); *Holes and Wizzil* (Nuffield Theatre, Southampton); *Top Girls, Mother Courage* (Watford Palace Theatre). Design for opera includes: *The Magic Flute* (ETO); *The Cunning Little Vixen* (Royal College of Music); *La Calisto* (Early Opera Company). She won Best Design at the 2007 TMA Awards for her design for *Small Miracle* by Neil D'Souza.

Helen Gaynor (Company Stage Manager)
Over the last thirty years Helen has worked in Europe, America and Australia, as well as the UK, where she has been employed on drama, dance and opera productions. Recent theatre credits include: *Feeble Minds* (Spare Tyre); *Pied Piper* (Boy Blue Entertainment); *Loot* (Tricycle Theatre); *Red Fortress* (Unicorn Theatre); *The Harder They Come* (West End and Barbican); *Carnival Messiah* (Harewood House, Leeds).

Lucy Morrison (Director)

Lucy is Clean Break's Head of Artistic Programme. For Clean Break, she developed and directed *This Wide Night* by Chloë Moss (Soho Theatre, Live Theatre Newcastle and Plymouth Drum Theatre). *This Wide Night* won the Susan Smith Blackburn Prize 2009. She was formerly Literary Manager of Paines Plough, where she worked with many of the country's most exciting playwrights, including Dennis Kelly, Abi Morgan, Sarah Kane, Chloë Moss, Mark Ravenhill and Jack Thorne. Her directing credits include: *Product* by Mark Ravenhill (Paines Plough at Traverse Theatre, Royal Court Theatre Upstairs; European tour including Schaubühne in Berlin, and theatres and festivals in Moscow, St Petersburg, European New Play Festival at Wiesbaden, and the Bush Theatre).

Lucy Kirkwood (Writer)

Lucy is an East London-born playwright. She won the PMA Award in 2006. She has been Resident Playwright at Clean Break for the last two years, during which time she developed and wrote *it felt empty…*, working closely with Lucy Morrison. Previous productions include *Tinderbox* (Bush Theatre) and *Hedda* (Gate Theatre). She is currently working on a Sloan commission about particle colliders for the Manhattan Theatre Club, a play on Sino-American relations for Headlong, a six-part TV series for Kudos and a screen adaptation of the anonymously written novel *Sabine* for Ruby Films/FilmFour.

Hara Yannas (*Dijana*)

Hara received her training at the London Academy of Music and Dramatic Art (LAMDA). Theatre productions whilst training at LAMDA include: the world premiere of *On the Boost* by Mark Ravenhill, *Passport to Pimlico*, *The Permanent Way*, *The Blue Room*. Other theatre includes: *Scrooge* (UK tour).

Madeline Appiah (*Gloria*)

Madeline trained at the Liverpool Institute of Performing Arts (LIPA). Recent theatre credits include: *The Crossings* (Theatre503); *Wealth* (Soho Theatre); *Arabian Nights* (New Vic); *Dionysus Unbound* (Bridewell Theatre); *The Wedding Dance* (Bolton Octagon); *Restoration* (Oxford Playhouse); *Cinderella* (Watford Palace Theatre); *I Have Before Me a Remarkable Document Given to Me by a Young Lady from Rwanda* (Dublin Fringe Festival – Nominated for Best Actress); *Brezhnev's Children* (BAC). Television credits include: *Doctors*, *EastEnders*, *Holby City* (BBC1); *Gavin and Stacey* (BBC3); *The Bill* (ITV1).

Becky Smith (Sound Designer)

Becky's recent sound credits include: *This Wide Night*, *Missing Out* (Clean Break); *Frozen* (Fresh Glory); *The Juniper Tree*, *Reverence*, *The Ghost Sonata*, *Visual Hallucinations* (Goat and Monkey); *The Moonslave*, *Johnny Formidable* (Punchdrunk); *Seven* (Arc Theatre). Becky also works as a Stage Manager and Workshop Leader and has worked with Oily Cart, Paines Plough, Top of the World, Schtanhaus, The Comedy School, Polka Theatre and London Bubble.

Anna Watson (Lighting Designer)

Anna trained at the Central School of Speech and Drama. Recent theatre credits include: *Rutherford and Son*, *Pub Quiz*, *Ruby Moon* (Northern Stage); *Glass House* (Clore Studio, Royal Opera House); *Something in the Air* (Oily Cart); *Sus* (Young Vic); *National Opera Studio Showcase* (Hackney Empire); *Twelfth Night* (Unicorn Theatre); *The Adventures of Wound Man and Shirley* (Contact Theatre Manchester and tour); *About Tommy*, *Richard III* (Southwark Playhouse); *King Pelican*, *Speed Death of the Radiant Child* (Drum, Plymouth); *Can Any Mother Help Me?* (Foursight and tour); *Salt* (Ruhr Triennale, Germany); *This Wide Night* (Clean Break, Soho Theatre and tour); *…Sisters* (Headlong at the Gate Theatre); *Torn*, *Mariana Pineda*, *Venezuela* (Arcola Theatre); *Nine* (ArtsEd); *Stumbling Over Infinity*, *Tongue Tied* (Linbury Studio, Royal Opera House); *Songs of Grace and Redemption*, *The Time of the Tortoise* (Theatre503); *Critical Mass* (Almeida Theatre); *View from the Shore* (Clore Studio, Royal Opera House/Hall for Cornwall); *The Persian Revolution* (Lyric Hammersmith); *The School for Scandal* (Salisbury Playhouse).

Rebecca Carnell (Deputy Stage Manager)

Rebecca Carnell trained at the Bristol Old Vic Theatre School, graduating in 2007. Since then she has worked for the Birmingham Repertory Theatre, Everyman Theatre Liverpool, and Curve Theatre, Leicester, on its first production in their studio space of *The Pillowman*. She also enjoys opera and this summer worked at Opera Holland Park on their production of *La Bohème*. She has also worked at Salisbury Playhouse, Regent's Park and most recently Bath Theatre Royal on *Another Door Closed* (Ustinov Theatre).

For *it felt empty when the heart went at first but it is alright now*

Production Team
Production Managers **Ali Beale** and **Rachel Shipp**
Company Stage Manager **Helen Gaynor**
Deputy Stage Manager **Rebecca Carnell**
Casting Consultant **Amy Ball**
Accent Coach **Elspeth Morrison**
Publicity Designer **Richard Scarborough**
Assistant Lighting Designer **Sunghee**
Production Electrician **Crin Claxton**
Costume Supervisor **Nicola Fitchett**
Trainee Assistant Production Technician **Renee Ge**
Design Assistants **Cecilia Carey**, **Alison McDowell**
    and **Helen Quinn-Goddard**

Marketing and Press Team
Marketing Consultants **The Cogency**
Press Consultant **Nancy Poole PR**

Lucy Kirkwood would like to thank the staff and women of the Poppy Project, especially Sally Montier, the Helen Bamber Foundation, Pierre Makhlouf, Mel Kenyon, the students and staff at Clean Break, especially Jessica Southgate for her assistance in researching this play, and Lucy Morrison, for her incredible support and collaboration.

Clean Break would like to thank the following for their support: the staff and women from the Poppy Project and Eaves; staff from the following organisations – Bail for Immigration Detainees, Music in Detention, Yarl's Wood Befrienders, Metropolitan Police Human Trafficking Team; Sus Jeffries; Professor Roger Matthews.

Clean Break

Clean Break is a women's theatre company set up by two prisoners in 1979 who brought the hidden stories of imprisoned women to a wider audience. Still the only company of its kind today, Clean Break has remained true to these roots and continues to inspire playwrights around the complex theme of women and crime. Integral to the company's artistic programme is our theatre-based education programme, which enables women in prisons, former offenders and those at risk of offending in the community to develop personal, social, professional and creative skills leading to education and employment.

Our artistic programme

Clean Break produces an annual production, based on an original new-writing commission by an established playwright, on the theme of women and crime. The production tours to theatres and prisons throughout the UK with the aim of engaging audiences and enhancing Clean Break's role as a social commentator on the subject of women, crime and justice. Over the years, we have worked with highly regarded female playwrights including Bryony Lavery, Winsome Pinnock, and Rebecca Prichard. In 2009 Chloë Moss's *This Wide Night* for Clean Break won the international Susan Smith Blackburn Prize.

Our education programme

Clean Break has been running its Education and Training Programme for over fifteen years, working with women aged 18–60 years. The programme is delivered at our purpose-built studios in Kentish Town. It comprises creative courses, financial assistance and specialist support, leading to qualifications, increased confidence and self-esteem, theatre and technical skills and pathways to further/higher education or employment. The programme aims to create a platform for learning and engagement for women who have not been in education for a significant amount of time, or whose experience of formal education was very negative.

Working in prisons

Clean Break has developed an expertise in delivering outreach work in women's prisons. Alongside the production tour, Clean Break delivers theatre and playwriting residencies and workshops within each of the prisons we visit.

Working with young women

The *Miss Spent* programme has drawn on Clean Break's expertise to develop a gender-specific arts programme meeting the needs of young women, aged 14–21 years, involved in or at risk of offending. Previously delivered in community settings, the programme is now being relaunched for young women in custody.

Make a donation and make a difference to more women's lives
Clean Break aims to bring about change directly in the lives of the women we work with and at a national level, by changing attitudes to women and crime through theatre, education and new writing. Our services are much in demand and we have ambitious plans for:

- more education work, affecting the lives of individual women and supporting them through their education at Clean Break and onto further or higher education, employment or voluntary work
- new-writing projects for former students of Clean Break and women in prison
- more commissions and touring productions focusing on women's experience of and relationship to crime, punishment and justice
- increased work with young women offenders and those at risk of offending
- training for artists and criminal justice professionals wanting to learn more about our ways of working

We invite you to contact us to discuss supporting one or more of these areas with a one-off or regular donation. We rely heavily on the generous support of our funders and donors. By making a financial contribution to Clean Break, you can make a difference to the lives of the women and their families. If you would like to discuss Clean Break's programme further and how you could get involved contact Lucy Perman MBE, Executive Director, on 020 7482 8600.

Alternatively you can donate directly online via our website at www.cleanbreak.org.uk

Clean Break
2 Patshull Road
London
NW5 2LB

Tel: 020 7482 8600
Fax: 020 7482 8611
general@cleanbreak.org.uk
www.cleanbreak.org.uk

Registered company number 2690758 | Registered charity number 1017560

Supported by
ARTS COUNCIL ENGLAND

Clean Break would like to acknowledge the generous support of all its funders and supporters.
Clean Break is a member of ITC

For Clean Break

Executive Director **Lucy Perman MBE**
Administrative Producer **Helen Pringle**
Head of Artistic Programme **Lucy Morrison**
Head of Education (maternity leave) **Anna Herrmann**
Locum Head of Education (Learning) **Imogen Ashby**
Locum Head of Education (Student Services)
    Jacqueline Stewart
Education Manager (Accredited Courses)
    Vishni Velada-Billson
Education Manager (Short Courses and Progression Routes)
    Tracey Anderson
Student Support Worker (maternity leave) **Ella Bullingham**
Locum Student Support Manager **Jacqui Ennis Cole**
Miss Spent Project Manager (maternity leave)
    Jo Whitehouse
Locum Miss Spent Project Manager **Charlie Weinberg**
Outreach Worker **Elvina Whitfield**
General Manager **Louisa Norman**
Development Manager **Elly Shepherd**
Company Administrator **Molly McPhee**
Office Administrator **Sam McNeil**
Finance Administrator **Won Fyfe**
Administrative Assistant (Education) **Esther Poyer**
Administrative Assistant (Artistic) **Amanda Castro**

Board of directors
Joan Scanlon (Chair), Sylvia Amanquah, Jude Boyles,
Rahila Gupta, Sonali Naik, Kate O'Rourke, Sharon Shea

Patrons
Paul Boateng MP, Carmen Callil, Dame Judi Dench,
Sir Richard Eyre CBE, Barbara Hosking CBE,
Baroness Helena Kennedy QC, Ann Mitchell,
Yve Newbold LLB, Baroness Usha Prashar CBE,
Baroness Vivien Stern CBE, Janet Suzman,
Emma Thompson, Harriet Walter CBE.

it felt empty when
the heart went
at first but it
is alright
now

Lucy Kirkwood

Author's Note

This play was created in close collaboration with the director and design team of its original production. We had a large warehouse space at our disposal, and the stage directions reflect this – I think it would be just as possible to produce the play simply in a single studio space.

The sections in which Dijana speaks in her native language can be done in any tongue you deem appropriate – but it may be of interest to know that in the original production, Dijana was Croatian, and that is represented in the text here. The women who fall prey to traffickers most often do because of their hope and ambition to improve their lives – this is often related to the wealth of their country, but not exclusively so, and while Dijana is statistically more *likely* to be Albanian or Moldovian, we felt this to be retreading ground covered elsewhere.

Whilst elements of *it felt empty when the heart went at first but it is alright now* are inspired by real-life events, all characters, their names and incidents portrayed are entirely fictitious. Any resemblance to the name, character or history of any person is coincidental and unintentional.

Characters

DIJANA, *Eastern European*

GLORIA, *West African*

Note on the Text

A forward slash (/) in the text indicates the point at which the next speaker interrupts.

This text went to press before the end of rehearsals and so may differ slightly from the play as performed.

PART ONE

You pay some money. You wait your turn. You are led into a room. You are given a letter. The letter is written by somebody who dots their 'i's with little hearts.

You are reading the letter when everything goes completely black. You cannot see your hand in front of your face. You hear bird wings flapping. The sound is all around you. It gets more and more frantic.

A scream. A loud, repeated thwacking sound. The flapping cuts out, and the lights come up.

You are in a modern, sparsely decorated flat. There is a copy of Cosmopolitan *magazine. There is a mug with a smiley face and the word 'Happy' on it. A pair of kicked-off pink high heels. A small fridge.*

DIJANA *is standing on a bed with a rolled-up newspaper. She is dressed in a miniskirt and a strappy top. She breathes sharply and deeply. Frozen like a child caught doing something naughty. There is a dead bird lying on the floor. She has just killed it with the newspaper.*

DIJANA. It wasn't me.

> *Beat. She scrambles down off the bed.*

> Don't be mad, shit, but, no but it flew in at the window and then it was flapping was frightened

> THIS IS SO NOT WHAT I NEED RIGHT NOW it

> could not go out again. Stupid bird. Sorry. You should not say bad of the dead but

> I try! Try to push it out with newspaper try to HELP IT, hello! but then it *fly*, it fly right at my face and so I

> panic and I

hit it and now is

dead. Is dead is dead on my floor and I am so so sorry. I am so sorry. But he should look where he goes!

She throws the newspaper in the bin and squats on the floor. Peering at the bird.

His beak… is broken. I broke it. I didn't mean.

Her face crumples. She starts to cry.

I think is a baby. It is so small. Oh shit. Oh God. Poor baby. Poor bird. I wish you did not see this.

She starts to brush at her arms, as if sweeping off invisible insects.

I am so sorry baby. This is horror to see. I wish you did not –

She stops suddenly. Shakes her head. Takes out a mobile phone and dials, pacing, one eye on the bird. Waits.

(*Muttering.*) Babac is not answering.

Hangs up. Rubs her head.

Shit FUCK.

She stares at the bird.

I am so glad I am out of here soon. I cannot fucking wait I tell you.

She picks up the bin, finds a plastic bag and starts counting out used condoms.

One, two

Three four five

Six seven

Eight nine ten eleven twelve thirteen fourteen fifteen

Sixteen

Seventeen eighteen nineteen

Twenty twenty-one

Beat.

Today is quiet. Usually, Saturday, special so close to Christmas, thirty maybe. Today? Only twenty-one.

Her phone beeps. A text. She looks at it.

Twenty-two. Ten minutes.

So twenty-two including next one, yes. Not so bad twenty-two. Maybe enough, twenty-two.

Beat. She takes out a small notebook and a pencil.

My maths it is very good. I have a head for numbers. Babac always say, You have a head for numbers Dijana Polančec. So. Twenty-one. Not including next. All fucks. So twenty-one times thirty is...

She writes the sum and works it out.

sixty hundred thirty UK pounds.

She pencils this figure in.

Plus two times fifteen for blowjobs plus five times ten for handjobs is

eighty add to six hundred thirty minus fifty for rent today and ten pounds for tissues and one hundred for maid is five hundred fifty profit, take this from monies outstanding...

She works it out, then writes in her calculation. Holds up the notebook.

I keep account. I keep account of money I earn very careful because when this number reaches twenty thousand UK pounds then I will have earned all the money I owe to Babac and he will give me my passport and I can stop.

I have earned already... nineteen thousand nine hundred and seventy pounds. So when I have earned thirty UK pounds more I can stop. That is the deal. When Babac tell me the deal I am like Oh! Yeah! Sure! Like I am gonna fucking trust you! Do I look like some IDIOT?! But I make it proper. We have a contract. I draw it myself and I make him sign it so yeah. It is all on paper.

I need only thirty UK pounds.

After next client I will have earned this.

So next client he will be my last.

Beat.

The next is the last.

Beat. This is a momentous thing to absorb.

So tomorrow I come to find you.

The first thing to do is to buy you chips and a swimming suit.

We are going to swim in the sea. I am going to eat chips in a car and swim in the sea with my baby. In Brighton.

She takes out a dog-eared, folded ultrasound image. Examines it.

I promise you. Can you hear me?

Knock once for yes and twice for no!

I wish I had other photos of you. Look how I have rubbed your face off. And you are so small here. You look like a fucking Heinz Baked Bean!

She laughs. Puts the print away. Then looks at her phone.

I better get ready.

She ties her hair up. We see there is a letter 'B' branded into the back of her neck. She picks up a foundation compact, wipes it round her face. Puts some lipstick on. Picks up a thong from the bed.

Babac gave me this. It is bit small for me, the girl before she must have been so thin. It's clean, I wash it really hot with soap. I have two others and also a bra.

She puts the underwear on under her skirt. She takes a big tub of Vaseline from under the bed and wipes some inside herself. Picks up two bottles.

Look. Babac did not give me these I took them by myself from bootsthechemist.

L'Oréal shampoo. And conditioner too. Because I'm worth it!

She pulls her hair out of its ponytail like she's in a shampoo advert and shakes her head in slow motion.

See.

But she doesn't laugh.

This is extra funny because I know exactly how much I am worth. How many people can say this! I am worth one thousand euros because that is how much Babac pay for me.

To put this in easy language, that is like two-and-a-half iPhones.

She puts the bottles back carefully, arranges them on the chest of drawers. Tidies the bed. Then sits on it. She stares at the bird. Thinking.

Something strange happen this morning also. This guy, he come and we fuck. Just normal him on top once then in my mouth and he come on my tits but after he go something weird, he go

Ummm… do you want me to call someone?

And in my head I am like Yeah do you have number of a dentist cos your breath stink.

But I do not say out loud. I do not say nothing.

But this guy he is still standing there and my next client he is coming and the guy he is looking all red and English like meat and he go Ummm you don't have to do this if you don't want you know.

And in my head I'm like Uh, okay it is like none of your business! Shit! Like I don't do what I want you know? I am fine. You think I stay here if I am not fine? I am fucking great mate! And anyway it is not like there are so many things I could do you know! It is not like I went to Oxford University or something!

Anyway I tell him, Today is my last day, *actually*. That shut him up!

He go, Oh.

Yeah I say, Tomorrow I will not be working here no more, which actually is true, I say I am starting new job in an office in the Canary Wharf, which is a small lie but who give a fuck right. I say Where do *you* work? We are not sposed to ask stuff like that but I am just like Fuck it today is my last day and he is been so nosy to me and tomorrow I am out of here so I say What is your job?

And he says I am a supplier.

And I am like Yeah. And I yawn, to show how boring he is. Of what?

And he says Pigs.

She raises her eyebrows.

Okay. And what do you supply to these *pigs*?

No, he say, I supply pork. I am a pork supplier.

And I start to laugh cos I think it is a joke, right? Like a shit joke, but a joke, but he don't laugh. He say

My business partner has a farm. In Glaus-ter... in Glauster. It is beautiful place. The pigs can go anywhere. It is open fields. There is apple trees. They eat. They sleep. They have long life.

And then you slit their throat! I say. I just try to piss him off now, I don't like him. It is right he makes pigs, his eyes are like a pig's they are small and close together and he blinks like there is flies in them.

The meat is so good he say. You should taste it. You would not believe. The difference in taste.

How much it cost I say. And he say a number and I laugh, I have a head for numbers and that is a fucking stupid price to pay for some bit of pig you can get it so cheap in Kingsland Road.

And he look sad then, and he go Our customers can afford it. Our customers believe to pay for quality.

Who your customers, I am shouting now I don't know why, What shop you sell this in!

Waitrose, he go. And then I am quiet so he say, It is a supermarket, and *that* make me MAD so I go YEAH I KNOW. And I am bored of this now and his time is over so I put my bra on and that tells him.

Good luck with your new job, he go, as he walk out.

I see he has forgot to do up his flies.

Beat.

Prick.

Usual the men I see are better than him. Usual they are very rich and high-class. And sometime famous.

And the *experience* is real high-class too. V... *exclusive* yeah? I make more money this way.

For example, when a man comes to see me, he must first allow me to wash his penis.

I know, it sounds not so nice!

But I do it very sensual. In the bathroom with rubber gloves on. And in this way we know the man is clean.

I am clean too. Babac take me to get tested in a clinic every month. By Pamela. She is so funny. She make me lie, like this...

She lies on the floor with her knees bent and together.

And then she say FLOP.

She flops her legs open, feet still together.

And then she say to me always, Dijana does this hurt? Every time, Dijana, does this hurt?

And I am like, What do you think? You have got big piece of plastic in my pussy!

She does not laugh at this but I know she finds it funny. Cos she keeps saying it like every fucking time.

Pamela is so nice but she is so *old* like about fifty years old so it make me laugh so hard when she says the word 'anal'! I always pretend I have not heard so she have to say it again.

So yeah I am pretty high-class.

She turns round and pulls her top off, leaving just her bra. Across her back are a number of large, violent, spreading bruises. At the base of her back is a tattoo reading 'Angela'.

I am like, what is her name, I am like – *Billie Piper*. High-class! She has a Secret Diary, it is so funny! So yeah, I guess I am like Billie Piper the most.

She pulls on a different top and turns back to us.

Sometimes I go to nice hotels. Four star! Or five. With minibar and small soaps you can take home.

I have even been with film stars!

Well. Men from the television, I do not know if they have been in the movies.

But definitely TV. Definitely famous.

I can't tell you who.

She bites her lip, tempted. Then shakes her head.

No! I must not say! Not even to you, little clown!

Pause.

I think Babac has new girlfriend.

I don't care or nothing. I am done with men! I just really like sex you know. That is why is okay this. I love it so much, sex. I am so modern. Babac can fuck who he wants. When I meet him for first time I think Oh man I am so in love. But I go off him now. And I am out of here tomorrow anyway! He can fuck who he wants. Is my choosing not his. I won't cry.

She shrugs. Brushes at her arms again. Sweeping invisible pests away.

I don't cry too much. It does not help fucking no one. I cry when you go. Sure I cry then.

Beat.

But since that time? (*Shrugs.*) I cry like… never. No, wait, shit, I cry once.

Cos what is was yeah this guy he come and we fuck and then he die. On top of me my face is squashed on floor by how heavy he is. Was horrible.

And Babac he sort it out, like he make the body go but in time I wait for him to come I just sit here with dead man. And it make me sad cos I see his wedding ring and I think of his wife and it make me cry. Thinking about police when they go to her, and say her man is dead. Questions she will ask.

Like, How he die? Was it car accident?

No.

Was he pushed under a train?

No.

Was he shot with a gun?

(*Shakes her head.*) No.

Well what his wife will say! You must tell me how did my husband die?

And they would say

Your husband die in Dalston fucking beautiful prostitute in the ass.

Beat.

It probably made the funeral a bit difficult for her.

But maybe they say something different. The truth it is very strong for some people.

It was strong for me! I cry then. When I sat there waiting.

Believe it or not my ass has never killed a man before!

Sorry. Is not funny.

Beat. She puts her hand to her mouth, and looks at the bird.

I just had such bad thought. Like if this bird was not a bird but a person that looked like a bird like a little boy or a girl and it was lost and flew in here and then I and then I and then I and then I and –

She starts to hyperventilate. She brushes at her arms. Frenzied, purposeful activity as she goes to the bin. Pulls out the newspaper. Spreads it on the floor, tips the bird onto the newspaper and wraps it up quickly, gagging, picks up the bundle at arm's length, marches to the fridge, puts the bird in and slams the door. A shudder – the feel of feathers on her skin – then she rummages in her handbag, can't find what she wants, she tips it upside down, the contents spill onto the floor – make-up, perfume and shampoo bottles, her notebook, a hairbrush, condoms, deodorant, cigarettes, tissues, and, falling in a flutter, many pictures cut out from newspapers and magazines of little girls. She ignores these, grabs the deodorant, sprays herself, then scrabbles for her lighter and cigarettes, lights one. She checks her phone for the time.

Shit. He is here soon.

She briskly starts repacking her handbag. Gathers the scraps of paper. Stops on one. Holds it up.

Look at this girl! She is seven years old!

She is youngest person in the country to have her heart transplant with another person's! They took out her heart and they put another one in because hers did not work properly.

She is really brave she is only seven. I bet you would not be so brave. But this little girl, she has her whole heart taken out and still she smiles for the camera and talks to journalists and when they ask How does it feel? she says

It felt empty when the heart went at first but it is alright now

Tubes up her nose she says something beautiful like that! If a journalist tried to talk to me when I had tubes up my nose I would tell him to go and fuck himself.

But maybe they gave her chocolate or something.

Beat. DIJANA *looks round at the fridge.*

I hope it does not come alive and start to fly round the fridge when client is here.

She shudders. Then looks at her phone. Busies herself tidying the bed.

A knock at the door. She quickly sits on the bed. The door swings open.

He is here! Twenty-two. The last man.

She waits as the client, invisible to us, enters. The door swings shut again. We hear footsteps.

He is old this one.

But he wears nice suit. Maybe Dolce Gabbana or River Island. That was nice of him, to wear a nice suit for such special occasion.

DIJANA'*s eyes follow him across the room as he walks to the bed.*

His legs are like a lady's, almost no hair at all.

The mattress indents with his invisible weight. Some banknotes drop on the bed.

He does not want to talk.

She lies down on the bed. Opens her legs. Turns her head to look at us as she starts to be fucked by the client. Her body jolts with his invisible movements.

His skin smells. Not aftershave. Not bad.

Just smells.

He keeps his eyes closed.

I hope he has a strong heart.

Pause. The fucking gets harder, faster.

What do I think about?

I think about tonight.

I think about if when I see my passport I will recognise my face.

I think about who is the girl who will be in this room tomorrow when I am in Brighton with you.

I think about the cracks in ceiling.

Harder, faster. She looks right at us. The sound of bird wings flapping from the fridge.

I think about washing my hair with L'Oréal because I am worth it.

I think about the pig man and shopping in Waitrose.

Harder, faster. DIJANA *closes her eyes. The flapping gets louder.*

I think about the wife of the dead man crying her heart out.

I think about how scared must have been the bird, to fly inside and not know how to leave again.

She is thrown onto all fours as the client fucks her from behind.

And then I can't stop it I think about you I think about you I think about you and how I have been waiting for this day for seem like always and now is here I don't believe I don't believe it ow.

And I think about how I will be in Brighton tomorrow and buy you chips and a swimming suit and then we are going to go swimming in the sea.

I think about what colour swimming suit is best.

I think about tomorrow ow.

I think about tomorrow and

I think about

I think about…

I think about nothing.

Her hair has been grabbed, her head is yanked back, her neck stretched.

Is better to think about nothing.

I think about nothing

and count to twenty-two.

Harder. Faster. Harder. Faster. Harder –

The bird wings suddenly stop. DIJANA *flops onto her front, her face against the bed, looking at us.*

Thank you. Have a nice day.

She lies there. Quiet. The door opens and closes. The man has left. She pulls two ten-pound notes and two fivers out from under her. She counts them.

Ten. Twenty. Twenty-five. Thirty. (*Beat. Again:*) Ten. Twenty. Twenty-five. Thirty. (*Beat. Again:*) Ten. Twenty. Twenty-five. Thirty.

She writes the number neatly in her account book. She checks her sums. She closes the book. She puts the book and the money in her handbag. Beat.

The enormity of this spreads through her. DIJANA *stands. She pours vodka into the 'Happy' mug. She downs it, staring at the fridge. Takes a deep breath. Gathers herself. Goes to the fridge. Takes out the bird. She walks to the window. She opens the window. She throws the bird out as if releasing it. She closes her eyes.*

Tonight that is me. Tonight I fly away. And in the morning I will be in Brighton. By lunchtime I will find you. For lunch we will eat chips in a car and then I will buy you a swimming suit. I wish you could hear me, little clown. I wish you could hear that tomorrow I will be with you but I hope you know more that I was always with you even when I was not I was always with you like when I wake in the night and I can't sleep sometimes I hear you breathe small sounds you make and then I could sleep then I could sleep because I think if I can hear you like this you can hear me too and if you can hear me you will know, you will know that I am coming and I have said this before but now is *true* –

Suddenly a vent falls from the wall. Wind whistling through it. The smell of the sea. A dark chasm big enough for a person to disappear into. DIJANA *opens her eyes. She goes to the vent. Puts her hand in. Takes it out. Sprinkles a handful of sand to the floor. Smiles.*

See?

I told you.

I told you I was coming. I don't think you believe me.

But now you see.

She picks up her bags. She climbs into the vent. And then she is gone.

The room is quiet. Then…

* * *

BA-DOOM BA-DOOM BA-DOOM BA-DOOM a heartbeat pulses in the air and GO GO GO GO you are pushed out of the space the building is being raided the police are coming up the stairs and their sirens wail and lights flash and you find yourself moving quickly and you notice that above you DIJANA *is scrambling through a tunnel, moving faster than you, speeding ahead through time and space –*

– and then you lose her but you keep moving and soon you find yourself in –

– a corridor. Doors on either side. It is lit above by electric bulbs but there is sand under your feet.

You come to a desk and there is a policewoman sitting at it and she doesn't seem to understand you but she shows you a child's swimming costume in a clear Ziploc bag. It still has the price tag on. And then she wants you to press your finger-tips into a pad of ink and you don't know what you've done wrong but you do it anyway and she takes your hand and she presses your fingers to the walls –

– and soon fingerprints cover the wall and the policewoman guides you on past her desk and now the sand is deeper but there's something else mixed with it, it looks like –

– hair and you can hear the sea, the waves crashing against the shingle beach. A breeze rolling up the corridor towards you. The smell of salt. Then –

A security alarm going off in the distance. And someone panting. Running. Breath getting quicker and quicker as they run faster and faster and then with one last gasp of air –

End of Part One.

PART TWO

It is suddenly dead quiet. You are in a long, long narrow room. The size of things in here seems all wrong. The walls are lined with doors of all sizes, too-big doors, too-thin doors, too-small doors. Exits all over the place but no feeling they go anywhere. Some things in the room seem larger than they should. Others smaller. It is a sterile, impersonal place. You are not meant to feel at home. DIJANA *sits on the floor.*

DIJANA. So Brighton is a dump huh.

When I am there it is pretty grey most time and the shops they are so expensive like three UK pounds for fucking cup of shit coffee and arcades of games I didn't like it.

But it was good when I found you. Then it was good.

I was so scared I cannot tell you, that you would not know me.

But you was so happy to see me! You would not let go my hand you was so happy. And how much we talked.

Not at first, you was quiet at first but then! You are a real little motormouth.

We did not get to swim in sea though.

I wish we had got to swim in sea. That is really annoying that we did not get to do that.

I did get you swimming suit though so maybe one day when I stop being here.

Beat. DIJANA*'s right hand starts shaking. She holds it still with her left hand. Waits for it to stop.*

When I earned twenty thousand UK pounds I showed Babac my account book and my sums and the contract and he laughed at me.

And I watch him laugh for some time and it is weird like I am outside my body, like I watch me watching Babac laughing like I am on the ceiling not in my body at all and then scream I don't know for how long but I scream and I bite him, I am hitting and biting Babac

And then pain at my head and everything go funny again, like underwater, like sounds get loud then quiet again, loud then quiet, and my hair catch in something and then I see what my hair is catch in is his hand Babac's hand and just after this is when I see Babac is bashing my head on the wall.

Everything go black then and I guess I go to sleep cos when I open my eyes later it is morning but early still dark and I hear a bird sing and I listen to him and I think about you because I always think about you when I wake up and I wonder how I am going to do it and what is more quick the pills or the razor.

Beat.

But you would not believe then what happened then.

There is a doorbell

and I pull myself to the window. And I see outside two men. And I guess Babac answer the door because then he is there on the path and they have his wrists in the cuffs and Babac is shouting and kicking but they hold him push down his head and into the car and then Babac is gone.

Later someone tell me they come cos he was doing fraud with credit cards. It is so weird how you can live in a house with someone and not know things they do.

They have gone so fast they have not locked the door.

I just walk out.

I just walk out.

I just

walk out.

And it is so scary for a minute.

I just stand in the street. On my own. In the street. Then I see the Christmas tree in the windows and remember I am cold so I go inside and take a big coat of Babac's from the hook and also my bag and then I go and then I am gone and I start to run and I keep running and I stop only when I get to the canal and I sit on a bench and light cigarette and the sky is no colour and I take deep breaths.

The coat smells of him and I am sick on the path.

Beat.

Last night I drive for so long in a car with three women and also some men. But there was cages to keep us apart so was okay. I did not have to touch them or nothing. And then in the morning I was here.

Beat.

In Brighton we ate chips, I had enough money for chips. Not enough money for swimming suit because it was like fifteen UK pounds but it was big shop and I know what I am doing and Babac's coat have big pockets and the swimming suit it is so fucking pretty and I know you would look so beautiful in it and what am I supposed to do put you in the sea in your fucking underwear?

It really is a big shop and part of a famous chain.

At police station, they were shits. Question they ask. The worst was woman police, she talk for like hours and I tell her everything again and then she go

You say you wanted the item for your daughter, Miss Polančec? And the man, he whisper something in her ear like I am not sitting right there, and *then* she go

Oh.

But she still say it again she say You claim you take the item for your daughter.

And I know she's got it there right there on the paper fucking, in front of her so what a stupid fucking question but I just say Yes.

Then there is a big quiet. And then she go You understand Miss Polančec, that you are against UK law?

Beat.

I say I don't know.

She say You don't know?

I say No.

Beat.

After I am sick I sneak in bendy bus and I sit outside Victoria Train Station with a cup and because I am pretty and cry sometimes I make thirty UK pounds about.

Then I got on another bus they call it Megabus but apart from that you can get on it for five UK pounds it is really not so great. And then I am in Brighton.

And for three days I am walking walking all day long and looking but no good.

And I start to feel bad like I have been so fucking stupid. To think I could just get on Megabus to Brighton and find my baby all so easy.

You cannot imagine.

You really cannot.

I am looking for so long and not finding you.

I am so tired I walk up the pier but my feet they are just dead meat and even though it is blue skies and sun I am feeling very black.

So you cannot imagine

You really cannot.

The surprise.

When I look down and you are standing next to me, up on the rail.

I am searching for three fucking days and there you are on the pier all the time!

Careful, I say to you, you are leaning over rail. You will fall in the sea and a fish will eat you.

You shake your head, No.

No what I say! You do not think the fish would be happy to find a tasty little dish like you? He would gobble you like that!

I click my fingers and you laugh. You have a bad haircut, like they put a fucking bowl on your head or something but your hair it is dark like mine.

I want to smell it.

You don't say nothing and I pretend not to be bothered with you no more and this upset you, you do tumbles on the floor, check with your little sly eyes if I see or not – yes I saw you! and I want to watch you so much but I stop myself till you roll at my legs and this is when I turn and I look at you and I gasp

My God, little clown I say. Where did you learn such amazing cool tricks?

You just laugh again and get back up on the rail.

We stand like this for a while and the wind comes off the water and it makes me feel so nice.

I look down, you are pulling a face

Careful I say, the wind will change and you will be stuck ugly like that for ever.

You don't stop so I pull a face back.

She pulls the face.

The sun go down now and the sky is pink and a man's wheels squeak as his wife push him up the pier.

And when I look down again my baby lies on the floor pretending to sleep!

You make little snores.

And that make me cry, cos you look like I always imagine.

And then you put your hand

into my hand

DIJANA's *face crumples.*

And it's so small, you know?

And then it is quiet for a long time

and then I say

Little clown?

Little clown?

I lean down and whisper in your ear my nose in your hair I can smell it

Little clown? I say.

How would you like to go swimming in the sea?

And you nod your head. And I take from my bag a packet of chips. The paper is still warm and your eyes go so wide. And I say to you Stay here. Eat. And by the time the bag is empty, I will be back. And I will have a present for you.

Beat.

It really was a massive shop.

They had a whole floor of new underwear.

Beat. DIJANA *looks down. Then* DIJANA *cries. An animal howl. Sobbing into her chest.*

I don't want you now.

Go away.

GO AWAY PLEASE.

I SAID GO AWAY I AM SORRY OKAY I AM SO SORRY
BUT YOU CAN'T BE HERE ALL THE TIME I am so tired
just

looking at me GO AWAY! Goawaygoawaygoawaygoaway I
CAN'T SEE YOU! I can't see you no more please go away!

GLORIA. Who are you talking to?

DIJANA *spins round. Freezes.* GLORIA *is sitting up in bed.
Nigerian. Far away up the other end of the room, on a ledge
high on the wall. We have not noticed her before.*

DIJANA. Nobody.

GLORIA. If you do not shut up, I am going to stamp on your
head.

She climbs from the bed. Stares at DIJANA. *Stamps hard on
the floor. It echoes.*

DIJANA *stares at her, terrified. Then* GLORIA *starts to
laugh.*

Only joking! Oh my life, your face!

GLORIA *moves up the room towards* DIJANA.

DIJANA. You said –

GLORIA. I did not mean it! Look at your face! I got you!

DIJANA *sinks to the floor.*

DIJANA. Yes. You got me.

GLORIA. I got you so *good*! HA! Do not sit on the floor there,
that is where I piss.

DIJANA *leaps up.* GLORIA *laughs again.*

I got you again! You think I do that! Oh shit, you think I am
an animal or something!

DIJANA. No. Please. / No –

GLORIA. It is okay. Chill. Hi. I am Gloria.

Beat.

You are Dijana right? This is your first day?

DIJANA *nods.* GLORIA *takes out a little plastic box from her pocket.*

GLORIA. Yeah I thought so. Me? One hundred twelve. Do you want a Tic Tac?

DIJANA *shakes her head.*

Take it. I am not being funny but

you got *breath.*

DIJANA *takes a mint. Puts it in her mouth. She feels in her pocket. Pulls out a coin. Holds it out.* GLORIA *looks at it.*

What is this?

DIJANA. Pay.

GLORIA. Pay?

DIJANA. For Tic Tac.

GLORIA *kisses her teeth.*

GLORIA. You do not got to pay. It is a *mint!* You do not got to pay!

Beat.

DIJANA. Thank you.

GLORIA *nods. Knocks back a handful of Tic Tacs.* DIJANA *takes out the small notebook from Part One and starts to write in it.*

GLORIA. What is this?

DIJANA. I keep account. I keep account because the lawyer say ninety/-six days –

GLORIA. They send you a lawyer already?

Beat.

DIJANA. Today.

GLORIA. Today? Oh shit. You are *lucky*. I have been waiting time. They never send me one yet. They send you one already? What did he say?

DIJANA. She say. When ninety-six days are over I maybe leave here and go somewhere else. I have been here one day.

She writes this in the notebook.

So in ninety-five days I can stop being here maybe.

She closes the notebook.

I have a head for numbers.

GLORIA. Is it?

DIJANA. Yes. Why are you here?

GLORIA. I chop off my auntie's head with a cleaver. She died.

Beat.

Shit, got you again! No, I am joking. I am the same as you yes. No passport.

DIJANA. I do have… I do have passport.

GLORIA. You just left it in your other bag right? Me too.

GLORIA *laughs.*

DIJANA. I DO HAVE PASSPORT.

Beat.

GLORIA. Okay. Chill. Where is it then?

DIJANA. My boyfriend. Somewhere. I dunno.

GLORIA. Oh right. Your boyfriend is it? My auntie has got mine. That is what I say to the police, I have not lost my passport, I have lost my auntie. They didn't laugh though.

Pause. GLORIA *takes a hairbrush and pulls it through her hair. Watching* DIJANA.

DIJANA. I am… sorry if I wake you.

GLORIA. You did not wake me.

DIJANA. You try to sleep.

GLORIA. I don't really sleep any more.

I have got… problem sleeping. Do you get me?

DIJANA *nods.*

Yeah.

Beat. DIJANA *takes a scrap of paper from her pocket, gives it to* GLORIA.

DIJANA. Can you tell me please. What does this mean? I ask the doctor to write it for me.

GLORIA. You see a doctor already? Oh shit you are so lucky!

DIJANA. Please. I don't know.

GLORIA. I'm just saying, you don't know how lucky you are! (*Reading.*) 'Cervical abnormalities.'

She looks up at DIJANA. *A recognition. Then hands the paper back.*

Yes. I got this too. It is your downstairs. Your privates. They did not explain it to you?

DIJANA. Babies?

GLORIA. No. Not babies. We have got enough problems without babies, right! Wait.

GLORIA *suddenly races back towards her bunk, climbs up to it, rummages under her mattress and runs back to* DIJANA *with something in her hand. She hands* DIJANA *a well-loved greetings card. It has a cartoon of a large pair of breasts in a pink bra on it.*

Here. My friend Nkoyo send it to me. She is in a town now called Nottingham. She send this card to me at my auntie's and I keep it in my knickers drawer. I look at it every day.

When I first read it, I laugh so hard some urine came out of me.

DIJANA *stares at the card.* GLORIA *continues, pointing out the words as she reads.*

I will read it to you. It says: 'A good friend is like a good bra. They both give you a lift.'

Beat.

It is a joke.

DIJANA. Funny?

GLORIA. Yes. So funny.

Beat. Then DIJANA *looks up at* GLORIA. *Smiles.* GLORIA *smiles back.* DIJANA *starts to laugh.* GLORIA *laughs too. They become almost hysterical together.*

Oh man, it is so nice to meet you! I am not just saying that, it actually is so nice to meet you. I don't like the others they put here before. They are all Somalian bitches. But we are going to get along so good! There were four of us at my auntie's. By six months, we were all getting our bleeding at the same time. Like the nuns!

DIJANA *laughs again. Then* GLORIA *takes the card back. Finds a pen in her pocket and scribbles on the card. She hands it back to* DIJANA.

Take it. It is yours now. I give it to you. See how I have changed the names? Do you see?

I have crossed out 'To Gloria, from Nkoyo' and written here instead, 'To Dijana, from Gloria'. And I have put one kiss after only because we are friends but we do not know each other very well yet. Maybe I will add more kisses tomorrow once I know you more.

Beat.

DIJANA. We are

friends?

GLORIA *beams at her.* DIJANA *is overcome. A pause. Then:*

Thank you.

A long pause. They look at each other.

GLORIA. They don't believe anything I say here. They think I lie. Ask me why I did not run away.

But it is only on maps Africa is a big country. People find you. My auntie could find me.

Like that, she could find me. And then…

They smile when I say the word.

JuJu. Little smile at each other. Like I do not see.

They think it is hocus-pocus. But it is real. There, a market there. You can buy what you want. Anything. A heart. Some hair. A breast.

Anything. Fresh tongue is one hundred thousand naira.

That is about four hundred pounds. A lot of money people can make from you, you see.

So it is not funny. JuJu. They should not smile.

I like my tongue to stay in my mouth, thank you.

DIJANA. Today is my birthday. I am twenty-two years.

GLORIA *beams at her. Then gently guides* DIJANA *to the floor.*

DIJANA. What are you –

GLORIA. Your hair it look like something die in it. I am going to brush it for you! Relax girl please!

DIJANA *tenses, her back rigid.* GLORIA *brushes her hair.*

See. It feels so nice doesn't it?

DIJANA (*quiet*). Yes.

GLORIA. Did he bring you here?

DIJANA. What?

GLORIA. Your boyfriend, did he bring you here? To
England?

Beat.

DIJANA. No. Babac was not who bring me here.

GLORIA. My auntie was who brought me. She not my real
auntie, you get me? I just call her that.

GLORIA *has pulled away quite a bit of hair. She looks at it.*

Oh shit girl! You are shedding like a dog.

Hey, it is okay. It will grow back right? Hey! You can have
some of mine!

Gloria will take care of you. Gloria is here now. Gloria will
be your momma.

Oh shit, this is so strange for you, yes? Yesterday you were –
where were you yesterday?

Beat.

DIJANA. Brighton.

GLORIA. Right, yesterday you are in Brighton and today you
are in this place with strange African lady. Talking about the
selling of breasts! Yes well. Welcome to England! You don't
need to be scared any more please. The Albanians next door
will try to steal from you, and the Somalians, the Somalians
are pigs do not talk to them. And the lady across the hall
keep trying to hang herself from her tights, but most times
she put it on to get attention so do not be scared. And if
anyone gives you a problem. Gloria will sort them. Anyone
touch you. Gloria. Anyone say something. Gloria. Anyone –
anything. Gloria. Okay?

DIJANA (*quiet, but smiling*). Okay. Gloria. Okay.

GLORIA. That's right! That's right! Gloria is your momma!
And what is this? A smile! That is better! Look at your pretty
face when you smile! Look at it! I could eat it you know!

*GLORIA wraps DIJANA in a fierce hug. DIJANA tenses.
Starts to struggle. Murmurs of discomfort. But GLORIA
holds her there until she calms, quietens. Then slowly,
DIJANA's arms creep up round GLORIA's back, until she is
holding her tightly too. Clinging on to her. They stand there
like that for a moment. Then GLORIA gently pulls away.*

Lights out now.

DIJANA. But… no.

GLORIA. But yes. You are tired little one. And I am here.

DIJANA. No. Lights on.

GLORIA. It is not allowed. I promise it is not so bad. And I will
sing you a song to sleep to.

*GLORIA turns off the light. The following occurs in the
darkness:*

See? Not so scary.

DIJANA. Lights on.

GLORIA. Shhhhh…

DIJANA. I don't like.

GLORIA. I sit with you till you sleep okay? / Come lie down.

DIJANA. LIGHTS ON.

DIJANA starts to cry, panicked, scrabbling for an escape.

GLORIA. I put the covers over you. Shh. It okay. / Gloria make
you safe. Gloria your momma now.

DIJANA. Please I don't like *lights off* I don't want I want

In the dark the sound of a struggle.

GLORIA. Stop now / you will hurt yourself –

DIJANA. Sići mene, ne popipati mene ne popipati mene to
mise ne svida – [Get off me don't touch me don't touch me I
don't like it don't –]

GLORIA. Shhh. / The wardens will come you must calm

DIJANA. Žao mi je na taj način žalostan ugoditi siči – [I'm so
sorry I'm so sorry I'm so sorry get off please get off –]

GLORIA. You must let your eyes get used to the dark. Let me
hold your hand –

*In the dark, the sound of a struggle. Animal noises. Canine
barking and growling. Two separate, non-English languages,
competing with each other.* GLORIA, *surprised, screams in
pain.* DIJANA, *frantic, hyperventilating.* GLORIA *turns the
light on. Blood on her cheek. A little around* DIJANA'*s
mouth. She has bitten* GLORIA.

What is wrong with you! Huh? What is the matter with you?

Silence. DIJANA *wipes her mouth and brushes the ants from
her arms.*

Hey! I said WHAT IS WRONG I ASK YOU A QUESTION
WHAT IS WRONG WITH YOU?

DIJANA. I don't trust you.

Pause. GLORIA *stares at* DIJANA. *Then she snatches back
her greetings card, and walks back to her own bed. Once
she's under the covers:*

GLORIA. Yes, well. I don't trust you either.

The moment I saw you, I did not trust you.

Beat. DIJANA *is sobbing quietly again.*

You better stop crying now. Pissing me off.

Sort yourself out before I turn off the light.

I got to sleep sometime you know.

Silence. DIJANA *stops crying.*

DIJANA*'s right hand starts to shake again. It gets more and more violent. She cannot control it. She holds her arm to steady it. She lets go of her arm. It shakes more violently. She waits for it to stop. Eventually it does. She is exhausted by it. She stares at the bed covers as she speaks.*

DIJANA. I am not sposed to talk to you no more.

The doctor says it's not healthy.

DIJANA *suddenly starts to choke, coughing. Eventually she brings up a tiny golden key. She stares at it. Then looks up. There is a tiny door in the opposite wall, the only one with a keyhole. She runs to it, unlocks it, it swings open. DIJANA kneels, crawls head-first into the space. And disappears.*

* * *

BING BONG BING!

The lights come on brightly and you hear the bustle of a busy airport terminal.

ANNOUNCEMENT (*in a variety of languages*). LADIES AND GENTLEMEN PLEASE MAKE YOUR WAY TO GATE SEVENTEEN, FLIGHT 793 IS NOW BOARDING!

And now GLORIA *is marching down the long thin room towards you dressed as an air hostess with a big air hostess smile and you are led by* GLORIA *along another corridor lined with clocks –*

– and you notice that the clocks are going backwards rather quickly and you go through passport control where they check your ticket and then you are ushered onwards –

– and there is a light at the end of the tunnel!

– and suddenly your shoes are wet and there are birds singing and you realise that you are in –

End of Part Two.

PART THREE

*A wide-open corn or wheatfield. The sense that we are in a huge
space of freedom and light. Dark green, lush hedgerows, and a
clear blue sky. There is a door in the horizon.*

*There is a standard lamp in one corner of the field. An arm-
chair. A small side table. A TV. A stereo.*

*Downstage there is a line of stuff, laid out, like one does when
packing for a holiday. A little wall. DIJANA's suitcase, upright
and ready. Bottles and tubs and tubes of suncream, hairspray,
deodorant, insect repellent. Books, mainly tourist guides. Tooth-
brushes, hairbrushes, phone chargers, coat hangers, a frisbee,
items she's added to over a period of days, like careful packers do.*

*DIJANA is hoovering the field. She is pregnant. Five months
gone. She wears a white smock-like dress.*

*Music plays from the stereo. She sings along. Dances a little.
Then: the sound of a plane roaring overhead. DIJANA turns off
the hoover, drops it and switches off the music. She runs to the
window, watches the plane go overhead. She feels her stomach.
Then points upwards. Excited.*

DIJANA. Did you see that! Shit. Did you hear it? That will be
me tomorrow! On a plane NEEEEEEEEEEOOOOO –
OOOOW flying away! (*She puts her hand to her belly.*) That
will be us baby!

We are going on holiday tomorrow! Babac and me and you!

We are going on a holiday.

On our holidays VACATION! I am a celebrity get me out of
here!

Babac take care of everything. Your daddy is so smart.

He book the hotel

He book the flight

He say Give me your passport, and I will take care of everything!

And he has! He has taken care of everything!

It is so easy. I just give him my passport and I leave all to him. I am a lazy bitch yes!

BUTOHMYGODIAMSOEXCITED!!!

Babac has not done no packing yet. MEN! What can you do! I tell him, I won't do it for you just cos –

Beat. DIJANA *looks down at her stomach. Rubs her hands over it.*

Do I sound weird? To talk out loud? Just… I want your English to be so good when you come out from there! And the doctor say I should talk to you… she say you can hear me and –

Can you hear me?

Knock once for yes and twice for no!

She laughs.

Okay. I am gonna think you can hear me. And so if you can, when you come out, you will know my voice and speak English like Princess Diana. Except not be in a car crash! Or make love with a Arab.

And if you can't hear me I am just mad fucking fat lady talking to herself!

You are gonna love the plane. I love the plane even when my ears go pop I love the plane. Last plane I go on, OHMYGOD, when I get off at London Heathrow, my cousin waits for me. I don't know him so well but he is so nice his name is Goran and he take me to his small house in Leytonstone and his wife make me instant cappuccino and say, Welcome to England!

She has many tea towels with cats on them.

And later Goran say Do you want to go out tonight? So we go to this club and inside at the bar already is Goran's friends and they say, Welcome to England! and Goran is friend with this one guy name Babac and he say, Welcome to England! I shake his hand and he kiss me on my cheek and then I am shy and sudden so tired.

Can you think how far I had come in one day!?

Music starts to fade in.

But soon the music is strong and I am dancing, I love to dance and the beats are good OH MY GOD I LOVE THIS SONG! And Babac buys me a drink and with a girl in the toilets I take a pill –

The music cuts and DIJANA *momentarily shifts her tone.*

I don't do drugs no more because of you and when you are born I will tell you drugs are bad and evil and you must not take them ever but this is a LIE because drugs are so fucking GREAT! They make you feel –

The music kicks in hard again and her tone changes back. She moves to the music.

Like your skin is prickles with happy and you melt to other bodies and your blood go fast and slow and normal I don't like strangers touch me but tonight I like their sweat on me legs pushes on mine, even hands on my bum I like it, I like strangers touch me –

I KISS A GIRL! AND I LIKE IT! HA! Only for fun just cos we are friends, I mean I will never see her fucking again but tonight, here we are like the best friends and we laugh so hard and dance and our hairs stick and I turn and there is Babac at the bar, he smile, he talk to my cousin but he smile at ME and his teeth are white in his skin, and that is when I realise I have taken off my top and I dance in just my bra! But not dirty you know, not to be sexy I was just hot I want Babac to dance too but Goran keep talking HE IS SO BORING!

And I make a face and Babac laugh his teeth are white he
has nice eyes, Goran still talk the floor is sticky the light is
bright his teeth are white my top is gone – I don't care I buy
another! – I am on a man's shoulders I stretch my arms the
beat is strong my fingers look long he give Goran money
Goran stop talking AT LAST I am high in the air I touch the
stars my body is beauty I close my eyes sweat run down his
teeth are white the light is bright I feel like free.

The music stops. DIJANA *stops moving. Breathless.*

Now I say in my head, when I think of Babac, I say I fell in
love with him teeth-first!

She checks her mouth in the mirror again. Throws it down.

And one week later cousin Goran have to go to business so I
move here with Babac. With your daddy.

It was July this month and so hot. And Babac buy me ice
cream. He buy me ice cream every day. Not just vanilla
flavour. Double Caramel Magnum. Every day.

And this is how I know. That he fall in love with me too.
And then there was you.

DIJANA*'s phone rings. She scrambles for it. Looks at it.
Puts the phone to her stomach.*

It for you.

Beat. Poker face. Then she grins and answers.

Only joking! Hello yes how can I help you?

Yes this is the right number.

*She cradles the phone in her neck and scrabbles through the
pages of a large red book. She finds a pen and takes the lid
off with her teeth.*

Sorry you say again please.

Right good. How long sir?

And what do you look for today sir?

Okay. Yes we can do. Home visit or…

Okay. What time you like please sir? If before five o'clock p.m. it is happy hour you get two for the price of one.

No. Okay she come at nine. May I have address please sir?

Yes… yes… yes okay. Sorry?

I see. Uh-uh. That is no problem. I am…

Sorry. That is

sad.

Beat.

Yeah. Okay. Without is twenty pounds UK extra but if you want is okay.

Yeah she do that. That without is also twenty pounds UK extra.

Yeah she do that. Yeah she do that.

Yeah she do that, okay, her name it will be Vesna, yes, you like her. No worries sir, have a nice day.

She hangs up. Starts finding another number in her phone. Puts the phone to her ear and waits.

He is poor bastard. He is in wheelchair. Life is a shit sometimes, hi Vesna?

The call has been answered. As DIJANA *talks she takes out the mirror, examines her mouth, takes another tissue and scrubs at her lips. Then throws it away.*

Kako ste? Kako je Danijel? [How are you? How's Daniel?]

Nemoj me jebat?! Ozbiljno? Dobro sam ti da je pizda! [You're kidding me? Seriously? This man is taking the piss!]

Okay yes Imam rezervaciju za vas – [I have a reservation for you –]

19 Ainsworth Road. Is Hackney. One hour.

Što? [What?] I don't know postcode. Why you want –

Sat Nav? You have –

Slušati, On je u invalidskim kolicima. Da, u invalidskim kolicima. Što? dobro ići i raditi u dućan onda! Devetnaest. Ne, *devetnaest*! [Listen, he's in a wheelchair. Yes. A wheelchair. What? Well, go and work in a shop then! Nineteen. No, *nineteen*!]

She hangs up.

Sat Nav.

She looks in the mirror. She examines her mouth. She takes a tissue. She rubs at her mouth.

When you are born I get new job. Babac can get someone new to do phones. I work in a office maybe. Or be an actress. I am so good at acting. That would be a cool thing to tell your friends at school yes?!

She throws the tissue away. Feels down the side of the armchair for something: a packet of cigarettes. She takes one out and sticks it in her mouth. Lights it. Opens the window and smokes leaning out of it.

Babac does not like me – (*She motions to the cigarette.*)

When we first are together, when I smoke he make big fucking fuss, like he pretend to cough and choke!

But now I am pregnant, he let me do whatever I want! Is so fucking great being pregnant!

She takes a drag on her cigarette and coughs. She looks at the audience. Guilty. Then she freezes. Overcome by an intense pain. She holds herself. Waiting it out. It goes. She reprimands her stomach, pretending to be angry.

Hey! Stop this please! Is only one. How you like I kick you so hard!

She quickly kisses her hand and puts it on her tummy. She gets up and opens the door. Peers out.

Babac? Baby?

No one is there, she shuts the door again.

Anyway

She takes a series of furious drags, feeling bad about it but wanting to savour it, then throws it out the window. Closes the window.

Is reward.

Today I do so much cleaning!

Hello and welcome to *How Clean is Your House?*

VERY CLEAN! Clean clean clean. I dust, I wash, I hoover. Today all I do is hoover! Hoover… ing?

She picks up a tattered book and flicks through it.

Yes. Gerund. Yes. (*Holds up the book.*) I learn so fast! My mama say to me, Learn English little clown and you will be master of your destiny! She did not say nothing about gerunds though. Hoovering. Yes.

I hoover here and I hoover there. In this room and

Another room. Another room not here. Maybe ten minutes on bus. Shoreditch.

She takes out the mirror and examines her mouth. Grabs a tissue and rubs at her lips.

Sorry. Just

checking.

She smiles. Plumps a cushion. Picks up a can of air freshener. Sprays it round the room.

So this is my crib!

Crib means house!

I think you are gonna really like it. I have made it so nice for you.

We have television made by Hitachi, we have stereo made by
A-iwa, we have (do not forget) hoover made by

She checks.

Hoover! Also many plug sockets. So many plug sockets!

There is like seven fuckin plug sockets in here. So many.

You know we are so lucky. We have so much.

You know I could say, anything I could say, like I want...

I want George Foreman Grilling Machine!

And Babac he would buy me

She clicks her fingers.

like that.

Babac he would buy me. Babac would buy me because he
love me.

Beat.

Maybe we should get George Foreman Grilling Machine.

*She thinks. Then takes out her notebook (her account book
from Part One) and writes this down.*

But I do not take the piss, you know? I am not stupid, uh –
trophy? girl. I did not come here to just like, sit on my ass! I
work! Totally I work I answer phones like all fucking day,
night sometimes too and it is easy but also you must be
organise like to, uh – cordinate? it. So yeah I collect monies,
I do accounts and stuff. Your mama she is flat out all day!

Sometime Babac say to me, You have a head for numbers
Dijana Polančec.

I never hear this expression before I think it is so funny. I
don't know why...

*She trails off and takes out the mirror again. Examines her
mouth. Scrubs at her lips with a tissue.*

Sorry. Sorry just I think I can see…

Something or… I dunno.

Like something.

She shakes her head and laughs. She throws the tissue away. Rubs her tummy.

What I saying? Before?

Oh! Yes, how good is Babac to me! Too good! Like, sometime I say to him Too much! You gotta stop!

And he is like Is okay you will pay me back someday but I know he joking because he kiss me on my head when he says!

He always kiss me on my head when he joking. Or when he has been pissed and shouted. Shouting?

She stops. Picks up her grammar book.

Shout-ing. Is gerund also. Most things with 'ing' are gerunds. Words you do with 'ing' they are gerunds.

Not fucking. I mean sometime gerund. When you do fuck, this gerund.

But when you say like, Oh that dress it is so fucking nice, that is not gerund.

I dunno what that is.

Just a nice fucking dress – (*She interrupts herself seamlessly and quickly takes out the mirror again.*) Sorry please but I worry I really think there is something. On my lip there is… something like a red…

Um… pozlijeda?

Or a… swolling or

I dunno. I just. I freak out a bit.

Shit. This morning you know, I tell you before I go to Shoreditch to clean the room which is so like NOT my job

but Babac says the maid is sick so someone gotta do it and…
What is, is I was doing the clean

I change sheets and I hoover floor and I tidy. Empty bin and
stuff. And I am about to do bathroom when *she* come out.
The girl who… in the room. And I feel bad about this.
Because I had never met one before you know because,
well –

she look like shit. And she go Hi and I go Hi and she go, I
never see you before and I go, Yes I know I am usual on
phones.

And she go, Yeah I used to do that.

Pause.

I don't think she understand me cos her English was like
even so fucking worse than mine, so I say it again like the
same thing but more loud so she understand.

NO. I ONLY WORK THE PHONE.

And she is so rude then she go Yeah I hear you stupid bitch.
And that is, you know, that is not cool cos I am like her boss
the wife of her boss – I mean not married, me and Babac we
are not married but soon. After you is born maybe!

And she just stand there. Smile at me. I don't like it. And she
go again. She go, I work the phones too she say.

Beat.

When, I say.

Like, one year ago, she say. When I get here.

From Jamaica, I say?

Fuck off she say. I am not Jamaican. I am African. I come
here from Uganda to work phone for Babac. And after I was
maid. You clean? I say. Yeah. I clean, she say.

Beat.

What, you hoover? I say.

Yeah I hoover she say. And clean the sheets and empty bin and tidy she say

And now, she say, Now I do this.

And she kiss me. On the cheek. She kiss me.

Beat.

I just left. You cannot have a sensible conversation with Jamaicans.

Beat.

When I get home I have bath very hot because I have pain and because this girl kiss me and I am scared to catch something from her.

She looks in the mirror. Examines her mouth. Scrubs her lips with a tissue.

Like AIDS virus.

Or face herpes.

She turns back.

I am being so stupid right? Only cos I think I feel a tingle and that is what the advert say when you feel a tingle buy Zovirax so maybe I should do that. Maybe we have? In kitchen, I check.

She exits, hurriedly. The sound of drawers clattering, off. She comes back in. Worried.

We do not have. I must buy.

Her phone starts to ring. She pulls it out, smiles at the name on the display. She answers it.

Hi baby! What? Yes I am just –

Tonight?

They come here?

What friends?

Okaaaaay. But baby I still don't feel so good.

Yes – same thing.

Yeah I know, is fine, is normal but baby – TAKE THAT BACK. TAKE IT BACK NOW that is shit thing to –

Okay. Sorry. I know, but baby what time is flight tomorrow?

Flight. Plane. Holiday. What time?

You don't know?

Well can you find this out please? Because –

Yeah, okay I am not – yeah I see you soon. Yeah I will. Yeah. Yeah listen –

I love you baby!

Baby I am losing y –

Baby?

Baby?

Babac?

She sighs in exaggerated frustration and hangs up. This is what girlfriends on the TV do.

He has got friends coming round! We go on holiday tomorrow and he has friends coming!

What friends, I said? You hear me say that right?

Just friends he says!

HA!

MEN!

RIGHT?!

Right! They get hairy but they stay little boys. I am so happy you are a girl baby!

But is okay he is scared sometime. My mama say *my* daddy was so scare when I come, he move to Russia! HA! Babac is so different though. He totally love his little spanner in the works! That is what he call you! How fuckin cute is this!

She takes out the ultrasound image from Part One.

Cos look, you do look a bit like spanner. If you do this:

She squints her eyes and stares at it.

A bit. I dunno. Who fuckin care right! Is cute.

She puts the image away, leans over and whispers to her tummy.

When you come I will get your name in a tattoo on my back. So you will be with me always. I pick the spot just here.

She lifts up the back of her top to show the area just above her leggings (where the tattoo is in Part One).

We make you in Brighton. Babac have business there. And I go with him. A day of vacation. Was fabulous! When you come out I will take you there and we will swim in the sea. I promise to you. We will swim and eat chips. The water is cold and delicious! Babac watch from pebble and when I run out he hold towel out for me and rub me dry and we eat chips in the car and we make love on back seat and the home of the seatbelt dig in me but I don't mind and after I just know, I know we had made you. And when the doctor tells me some weeks later by how long I am pregnant I work out the sums and I know I am right.

I told you I have a head for numbers!

So yeah. I think this day in Brighton was the time I was the most happy in my whole long life.

Beat. DIJANA *stares out the window. Enjoying her memory.*

I still think on your name. Maybe Margaret. Or Miquita. And Angela I like too. I cannot decide. You know I am so bad at decisions! It make me so stress! So I ask Babac this morning, he is no help, he say it stupid to name baby before it come out. You will have to stay inside, that way I will not have to choose!

She leans over and talks to her stomach.

How you like that, little clown! You stay there for ever in me!

DIJANA *is hit by another intense pain. She freezes, waiting it out.*

Little clown not like that very much! So.

The pain goes. She takes a breath. Smiles.

So maybe I ask the audience! (*She laughs.*) Hey, you know how cool it would be to go on programme like this? To be the one who sits in the big black chair and all my make-up done and to be the one to say…

THERE IS CASH IN MY ATTIC!

Beat. DIJANA *laughs.*

No, I am joking, joking, is wrong show! Wrong show. I know this!

I WANT TO BE A MILLIONAIRE!

She laughs.

And then we know all the answers and win all the money. That would be so cool yes? Then Babac and me we never have to work we just lie in bed all the day and listen to Capital Radio and do sixty-nines and eat Double Caramel Magnums.

DIJANA *takes the hoover out. Comes back in. Beat. She smiles. Bites her lip.*

This gonna sound weird yes?

But I need to tell you. I have to tell someone. My heart feel like it gonna burst.

She sits. Holds her bump. Speaks softly. Telling a secret.

What I want to say is. I never really like it before, you know

…sex

I mean I like it yeah I guess it was okay I get off and everything but with Babac is so

different is so…

Like I get wet for him!

She clamps her hand over her mouth, enjoyably outraged at herself.

It is so bad to say that right! Special to you!

No but serious I just *think* about him, just THINK and here inside me is, you know, is like wanting like

…fizzy! Like Alka-Seltzer in my pants! And like I love

how heavy he is

on me and I love

how safe I feel

holded on the bed, he is on top of me

and I love

the smell of him. The smell of him drive me crazy!

This is so gross but… when I put his shirts in the machine I put my face in them first, in the armpits!

Beat.

I just. I never felt this before.

I just want him. And I don't know no way to say it but

She speaks rapidly in an Eastern European language, explaining exactly what she means in a way that satisfies her for the first time. Then stops. Relieved to have said it at last.

Beat. DIJANA *laughs.*

I wish I could say it so you understand!

I wish I could.

And I know this sound like I am like, so full of myself, but I love also how much I can be proud of myself.

Cos I *make* this happen. This morning, when I give my passport to Babac, I look at it and I think

WOW!

how much has happen since I last went on the plane! I never done nothing brave in my whole fucking life before and maybe I still be stuck in shit-smell apartment married to fucking coach driver but I save my money so hard and I book the ticket. And I be brave. And I come here. And I am scared but also I hope. And I meet a man. And I fall in love. And I make you! And I learn the language better and better. And now the man who sell Turkish sweet on Kingsland Road know my name. And I work. And I have Oyster card. And I have iPhone! With Apps! And I make my life. And I am so

so

happy.

Beat. A door slams somewhere else in the building.

(*Under her breath.*) Babac! Babac is home. (*Loudly.*) HI BABY!

She gets up. She takes out the mirror. Fusses with her hair. Scrubs at her mouth. Rushes to the door. As she turns away from us, we see there is now a little blood on the back of her dress, where she has been sitting on it. A spreading stain.

She's about to open the door but stops. Smiles. Turns back.

You know. He think I not see but

he put my passport in the safe. With all the monies.

When I see that it almost make me cry.

He put it in the safe to keep me safe.

And then he make me a vacation. Just like that! I don't know you can go on a plane when you are so full of baby as I am.

But Babac say is fine. I say, How you know! And he say he call NHS fuckin hotline okay! So you see, he take care of everything.

Another painful twinge. She grits her teeth.

Hey you calm down in there please!

No more talking now.

It is getting late. You must sleep.

Tomorrow we are going on holiday.

Tomorrow we are flying. On a plane.

I tell you, you will love it.

She smiles. She makes gestures like an air hostess.

The exits are here

here

and here!

This last one is the door. She pushes on the door handle. The door will not open. She is surprised.

She tries it again. Leans her weight on it. She bends down. Looks through the keyhole.

Babac?

She moves back and rattles the handle. DIJANA *bangs on the door. Laughs.*

Babac! Stop talking to your friends and come rub my feet!

She bangs again. Then again. Then repeatedly. Feeling that her panic is irrational but feeling it nonetheless.

Then she stops. Listens. Tuts. She takes out her phone. Dials.

After a moment we hear a distant ringtone. But the call is not answered. She frowns. Shrugs. Hangs up.

She takes a fresh tissue. She scrubs at her mouth. Hard, rubbing it raw. Distressed now.

I feel a tingle. I definitely feel a tingle.

DIJANA *throws the tissue down. Walks to the window. Strokes her stomach absent-mindedly.*

You know. If the day is clear, you can see the Canary Wharf from here.

And the light that blink on the top.

This is where the business people work.

I think one day maybe I work there too.

Beat.

I have a head for numbers you know.

A lighting change. The packing is now lit to form the shadow of the London skyline on the wall. There's the Gherkin, the London Eye, the Houses of Parliament, Canary Wharf. Seats of money and power. Places full of tourists and men in suits, with money to burn and wives that don't understand them.

DIJANA *looks out the window and the shadows get longer and longer, eventually not resembling a skyline at all, instead appearing as nothing so much as a spreading, shapeless, enveloping darkness.*

Somewhere, a starling is singing.

The End.

A Nick Hern Book

it felt empty when the heart went at first but it is alright now first published in Great Britain as a paperback original in 2009 by Nick Hern Books Limited, The Glasshouse, 49a Goldhawk Road, London W12 8QP, in association with Clean Break

Reprinted 2010, 2011, 2012

Cover image copyright © jsmonzani.com
Cover designed by Ned Hoste, 2H

Typeset by Nick Hern Books, London
Printed in the UK by CPI Antony Rowe, Chippenham, Wiltshire

A CIP catalogue record for this book is available from the British Library

ISBN   978 1 84842 081 6